BRITAIN IN OLD PH

CAMBRIDGE

CHRIS JAKES

SUTTON PUBLISHING LIMITED

Sutton Publishing Limited
Phoenix Mill · Thrupp · Stroud
Gloucestershire · GL5 2BU

First published 1996

Cover photographs: front: St Andrew's Street, 1911; back: passing through Jesus Lock, 1894.

British Library Cataloguing in Publication Data
A catalogue record for this book is available from the British Library.

ISBN 0-7509-1230-8

Typeset in 10/12 Perpetua.
Typesetting and origination by
Sutton Publishing Limited.
Printed in Great Britain by
Ebenezer Baylis, Worcester.

For those who believe in, support and use public libraries,
in Cambridgeshire and elsewhere.

C.E. Brock, one of the famous family of Cambridge artists, produced this sketch of the Free Library reading room to mark its jubilee in 1905. It shows the wide variety of user; from town and gown, the young and the old, the professional and the artisan; and also that the female visitor sat at 'ladies only' tables.

CONTENTS

The crowd on Senate House Hill, which had gathered to see the University vote on whether degrees should be awarded to women, 21 May 1897. Photographers came to record the event, and the police to see that the undergraduates did not become too boisterous.

INTRODUCTION

Cambridge is a place that is known to many. Millions of tourists visit every year, and thousands come to study at one of the two universities, at the state and public schools and the language schools. However, Cambridge is also home to 100,000 people who live, work, raise families, shop, socialise and eventually retire here.

The city is ancient. The Romans built a significant town here (*Durolipons?*) on a site that was already occupied. The Saxons, Danes and Normans built, destroyed and rebuilt in their turn. It was the county town, the seat of government and an important trading centre before the first scholars came here at the beginning of the thirteenth century.

Yet today it is the legacy of those early medieval scholars, the University of Cambridge, growing steadily and more confidently from the foundation of Peterhouse in 1284 to the thirty-one colleges we know, that draws people to the city; to look, to wonder, to dream, to study, and not least, to photograph.

This volume looks at the town of Cambridge (it would not become a city until 1951) through the eyes of the photographer from the 1850s to the 1930s. The emphasis is with town, rather than with gown, although the University is not, and cannot be, ignored. Another volume in this series is to take a more detailed look at the University.

The Cambridge of the 1850s had a population of under 30,000. Chesterton, Cherry Hinton and Trumpington were separate parishes, divided from the town by the river or by open fields. The Market Square had only recently been enlarged, and the railway station, not yet ten years old, was an inconveniently long way from the town centre. On a restricted franchise, the elections were still open to corruption. Living conditions for many townspeople were dreadful, in overcrowded slums without proper water supply or sanitation. The River Cam was an open sewer.

HRH Prince Albert was Chancellor of a University made up of seventeen colleges 'devoted to the study of learning and knowledge, and for the better service of the Church and State', which in 1851 had a total of 1,760 undergraduates.

By the eve of the Second World War the town's population had risen to nearly 80,000 and Newnham, Chesterton, Cherry Hinton and Trumpington had all been brought within the town boundary. Housing conditions, water supply and sanitation were all greatly improved. The changes at the University had been even more dramatic. An undergraduate of the 1850s may still have recognised some of the buildings and customs but the style of teaching, breadth of subjects, facilities and professionalism had all altered for the better.

The majority of the photographs used are from the Cambridgeshire Collection, the local studies department of Cambridge Central Library. It exists to collect, organise and make available to the public material relating to Cambridgeshire and the Isle of Ely. The collection also holds the photographic archive of the Cambridge Antiquarian Society, which had the foresight to actively compile a photographic buildings record for all the towns and villages in the county between the wars. Today this work is being carried on by the Cambridgeshire Local History Society, which is organising the rephotographing of the villages covered by the original survey sixty years ago.

Photographs form an invaluable part of this county's heritage, and I would appeal to all photographers, professional and amateur, and to collectors of postcards or photographs, to consider depositing copy prints or negatives of their work in one of the county's local studies collections. Time passes, memories fade, and our towns and villages are changing week by week. If you enjoy looking at 'old' photographs, consider the interest and enjoyment someone may gain from your work in twenty, fifty or a hundred years' time.

The first, and largest, section of this book looks at the town, its people and its buildings over eighty years of change, starting from Huntingdon Road in the north and progressing to Trumpington Street in the south and east along the Newmarket and Mill Roads. Section Two follows the River Cam through the town, looking at its commercial and recreational life, and the buildings which line its banks. Section Three takes a look at the University, its social life and customs. The impact of the First World War on Cambridge is covered in Section Four. The final section takes in those communities drawn into Cambridge as the boundaries were extended, first in 1912 and again in 1934: Newnham, Chesterton, Cherry Hinton and Trumpington.

It is always difficult to decide what to include and what to leave out in a volume like this, and I have tried for the most part to include images not previously published. I hope there is something here for everyone to enjoy, whether a lifelong citizen of Cambridge, a student here for all too brief a time, or a visitor wishing to take away memories of an earlier Cambridge.

C.R.J.
Cambridge
September 1996

SECTION ONE

THE TOWN

The Gothic fountain on Market Hill, c. 1900. Built in 1855 when the market was laid out in its present form, it remained unchanged until the top was removed in 1953.

Huntingdon Road, looking north, *c*. 1910. This is part of the Roman road along which the town has developed. The Wheatsheaf public house is on the left.

M.E. Eley, hairdresser and tobacconist, occupied one of the cottages next to the Wheatsheaf in 1939. The barber's pole, tobacco signs, and the Rex Cinema advert all brighten up the front of the shop.

The Misses R.J. and E.W. Warboys' grocer's shop at 43 Castle Street, 1880s.

Ye Olde Three Tuns on the other side of Castle Street, c. 1910. In spite of being established in the sixteenth century, and being visited by Dick Turpin later, it was demolished in 1936.

The Assize Courts on Castle Street, seen here about 1900, were opened in 1842. The last surviving stone part of the castle, the gatehouse, had to be demolished to make way for them. A guide book of the time described this as 'a ruthless piece of vandalism and a cause of great regret to all lovers of antiquity'. The courts themselves were pulled down in 1953.

The County Gaol from Castle Hill, 1880s. The first stone, laid in October 1802, had come from the old castle and had been found while digging the foundations. A treadmill, to discipline the prisoners and grind corn, was installed in 1821. The gaol was closed in 1916 and the present Shire Hall was built on the site in 1931, using bricks from the gaol buildings.

HM Prison staff, Cambridge, December 1913. This group photograph was taken outside the Governor's office. Back row, left to right: A. Hills, W. Collins, H. Dobbs, J. Collinge, H. Bentley, F. Pullen. Middle row: H. Andrews, E. Taylor, Miss Mapston, Miss Woods (Matron), Miss Anderson, C. Styles, E. Carter. Front row: Mr Pead (Chief Warder), Mr Croxall (Clerk and Schoolmaster), Revd F. Hird (Chaplain), Mr Dobson (Governor), Dr Ezard (Medical Officer), Revd H. Whitehead (Deputy Chaplain). The names of the two cats are not given. A month before, on 4 November, the last person to be executed at the gaol, Frederick Seekings, was hanged by T. W. Pierrepoint.

Shelly Row, October 1937.

This thatched barn in a farmyard off Shelly Row, seen at the end of the last century, is said to have been used to lodge French prisoners during the Napoleonic war.

St Peter's church, seen from Kettle's Yard, 1937. Originally much larger, the church was reduced in size in 1781 and now only the tower and part of the nave survive. Jim Ede moved into the cottages on the right in 1957 and began their transformation into the Kettle's Yard Gallery.

Honey Hill looking down into Northampton Street, *c.* 1900. And what more appropriate name could there be for the pub than the Bee Hive, kept at this time by James Halls.

The corner of Magdalene Street and Northampton Street, 1904. On the right is W. Collin's timber yard, which made the road very narrow at this point.

The same junction in 1937. The timber yard has gone, the first traffic lights in the town were installed here in 1927, and in November 1936 the Folk Museum opened in the former White Horse Inn.

Kettle's Yard from Northampton Street, 1904. The Spotted Cow was kept by Henry Humphreys. The washing belonged to one of the nineteen different families living here at this time.

Magdalene Street, 1860s. Magdalene College, on the right, occupies the site of Buckingham College, a monastic house suppressed by Henry VIII. At the instigation of Lord Audley the new college was founded and the name changed. The common pronunciation of this, Maudlin (M'Audley'n) preserves the link with him.

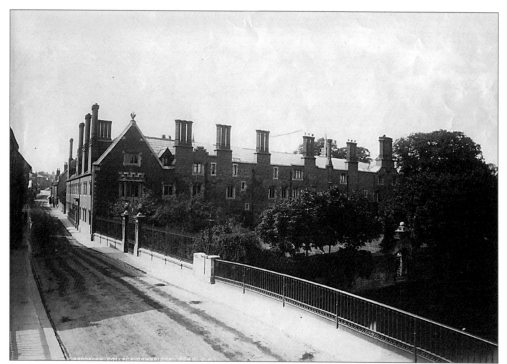

The Great Bridge over the Cam, and Magdalene College, 1890s. The buildings occupying the garden site, seen in the top photograph, were cleared in 1873. Today the water gate and most of the trees have gone.

Quayside from the Great Bridge, May 1910. The quay looks decayed and neglected, but it had not been that long since commercial boat traffic unloaded here, rather than the pleasure boats shown.

Workers at William Potts' Anchor Brewery, Quayside, 1880s. He owned the brewery from the mid-nineteenth century until 1895, when it passed to the Star Brewery. It was to close in 1902.

Bridge Street from opposite the Round Church, *c.* 1906. The left-hand side of the street would be pulled down to make way for new St John's College buildings in 1938.

The corner of Bridge Street and St John's Street, just prior to demolition, 1938. The premises were occupied at this time by the Singer Sewing Machine Co., Shallini, lingerie specialist, R.B. Darkins, newsagent, and H. Langdon and Co., builders and decorators.

Looking north from the tower of St John's College chapel, 1890s. In the foreground are the college Master's Lodge and Bridge Street, then Magdalene College and Street, St Giles' church and Castle Street, and in the distance the county gaol.

Jordan's Yard, 1939. This was one of the many yards which ran off Bridge Street. Through the archway over the fence can be seen the new St John's College buildings, and above, the chapel tower.

Holy Sepulchre church, 1860s. One of four round churches in the country, it was built in the twelfth century and much restored in the 1840s. Finding it too small for their growing numbers, the congregation moved to the redundant church of St Andrew the Great in 1994.

Bridge Street, *c*. 1880, showing the premises of Flack and Sons, bootmakers, W.H. Young, watchmaker, R.W. Dyball, billiard table proprietor, H. Thompson, bedding manufacturer, R. Saberton and Sons, tailors, and in the distance the Hoop Hotel.

Jesus Lane, 1894, showing the junction with Park Street and, on the corner, the caretaker's cottage for the Society of Friends Meeting House, taken down that year. Adjacent to this is the Royston Arms Hotel.

The cast of *The Roundabout* in the ADC Theatre, May 1935. The theatre had been badly damaged by fire in November 1933, and this show was put on in aid of the building fund. Left to right: Sheila Grundy, Molly Vintner, Donald Beves, George Rylands, Molly Roberts, John Roberts, -?-, Valentine Chapman.

Sidney Street, *c.* 1920. In the foreground on the left are Galloway and Porter, booksellers, and A. Wehrle and Sons, watchmaker, and on the right W. Stockbridge and Sons, antique dealer, Moore and Co., tobacconist, and John Johnson and Sons, tailors.

Sussex Street, off Sidney Street, was redeveloped in the 1930s. Work had begun in 1930 and this view was taken in 1938, the year the north side was completed.

Hobson Street, opposite Sussex Street, 1939. The premises of Frederick Morley, pawnbroker, are in the foreground and those of Cyril Ridgeon, builders' merchants, are next door.

The Central Cinema, Hobson Street, c. 1928. Opened in a former garage (see page 103) in August 1921, it was to show the first talking picture in Cambridge in August 1929 – *The Broadway Melody*. The following year this building was demolished and a new Central opened on the site.

Market Street, early 1880s. An absence of traffic allows the photographer to make a record of the building on the left before its demolition, and also to attract an eager audience who pose with a varied degree of casualness.

Holy Trinity church and Market Street, *c.* 1887, after the Henry Martyn Memorial Hall had been built on the site opposite.

Market Street and Market Hill, *c.* 1900. On the corner is the National Telephone Company exchange with poles and numerous telephone wires visible on the roof. It began business in 1892 and installed a trunk line to London in 1896. In 1909 the exchange moved to Alexandra Street.

Hobson's Conduit in its original position on
Market Hill, where it supplied fresh water
from 1614 to 1855. It takes its name from
Thomas Hobson, the carrier, of 'Hobson's
Choice' fame, who left money for its
upkeep in his will. It was rebuilt in
Lensfield Road in 1856.

Market Hill and Great St Mary's church, 1880s. Forty years before this, most of the open space was
occupied by a block of houses separated by Pump Lane from other buildings attached to the east end of
the church. The Conduit stood approximately where the cart stands. In September 1849 many of the
properties were destroyed by fire, and afterwards the opportunity was taken to demolish the rest and
enlarge the market.

The final parade of the Headquarters Companies of the 3rd (Cambs) Volunteer Battalion Suffolk Regiment on Market Hill, Sunday 29 March 1908. The Volunteers, under the command of Lieutenant Colonel B.W. Beales, were to be replaced by the new Territorial units, and had begun life in 1860 as the Cambridgeshire Rifle Volunteer Corps. Large local employers, such as the Cambridge University Press, often provided enough men to form whole companies.

The east side of Market Hill from the tower of Great St Mary's church, *c.* 1916. Left to right: Freeman, Hardy and Willis, Boots, the Great Eastern Railway Co., Victoria Cinema, Beales Patrick and Co., W.C. Green, the Wheatsheaf Inn, and Hallack and Bond. The Victoria Cinema had originally opened as the Electric Theatre in 1911, but had reopened under its new name in July 1915.

Crowds around the fountain watch folk-dancing in period costume, prior to the proclamation of a Tudor Fair, 27 April 1938. The fair, held in the Corn Exchange over three days, was to raise funds for the Church of England Waifs and Strays Society Harvey Goodwin Home.

'What about a pup, my boy?' People pause to see if A. Thurston has sold one of his puppies, or perhaps a tortoise, from the back of his converted hearse on Market Hill, in May 1936.

In February 1938 a photographer took the trouble to record the different stalls trading on the market, not knowing that within two years the war would put an end to such variety and choice.

A butcher preparing meat, with a fine display of joints on the trestle behind.

In August 1907 the third Esperanto Congress was held in Cambridge, with the inventor of the language, L.L. Zamenhof, attending. Here crowds gather in front of the decorated Guildhall. The police were given secret lessons in Esperanto so that they could manage the hundreds of visitors. 'Bonvenon al Kembrigo, plaĉa urbo en kiu, loĝi kaj labori.'

The Mayor and Corporation gather in the large hall of the Guildhall to witness the proclamation of King George V, 10 May 1910. At the organ is the tall figure of Alan Gray, borough organist, who accompanied the singing of the National Anthem.

The new Victoria Cinema, which had opened in August 1931. The advertised film, *The Vulture*, played for one week in October 1937. The films at the other Union Cinemas in Cambridge, The Central, Tivoli, Theatre Cinema and Playhouse, are also being advertised.

The interior of the Victoria Cinema showing the Christie organ, which was overhauled and repaired in October 1937.

Peas Hill, 1904. Later that year the premises of E. Bell and Son, corn merchants, behind the water pump, were to be gutted by fire and then demolished.

The market on Peas Hill, c. 1900. In 1579 the fishmongers on Market Hill were moved to Peas Hill, and the fish market was to remain there until 1949.

St Edward's Passage, 4 March 1935. In the foreground building work is in progress for the Arts Theatre, and in the middle distance people are browsing at David's bookshop. Gustave David, born in Paris, and known to all as David, came to Cambridge in 1896 and managed a bookstall on the market-place, and later this shop. He was to die in 1936, the year the Arts Theatre opened.

The first gala performance at the Arts Theatre was given by the Vic-Wells Ballet on 3 February 1936. The ballet dancers included Robert Helpman and Margot Fonteyn. Two years later, in May 1938, the company returned, and Helpman and other members of the Ballet are seen here at an art exhibition at the Gordon Fraser studio.

St Mary's Court, off St Mary's Street, 1938: a convenient place to leave your bicycle, and somewhere else to browse through second-hand books.

A postman collecting mail at the Rose Crescent post office, *c.* 1930. The buildings were constructed in the former yard of the Rose Tavern in the 1820s. An ancient inn, the Rose had been visited by both Samuel Pepys and Louis XVIII, King of France.

An aerial view north across the town centre, June 1934. The University buildings are sandwiched between the town and the River Cam. In the foreground are Corpus Christi College, the New Museums site, the Corn Exchange and the Lion Yard. In the centre are King's College, the Senate House, Peas Hill, the Guildhall and Market Hill, before the redevelopments of the late 1930s. In the distance, looking beyond Trinity and St John's Colleges, Bridge Street and Castle Street, can be seen the castle mound and the newly built Shire Hall.

Trinity Street and All Saints' church, *c.* 1855. Apart from St John's College in the background everything here would disappear: the wall in front of Trinity chapel in 1855, the shops opposite in 1858, to be replaced by Whewell's Court, and All Saints' church, closed in 1864, and sold by auction and pulled down in 1865.

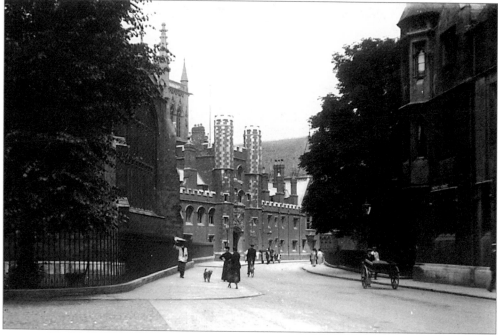

The same view some fifty years later, showing the street widened after the removal of All Saints' tower. The kitchen porter, carrying a meal to an undergraduate's lodgings, seems to have attracted the attentions of two dogs.

Matthew and Sons' shop undergoing alterations in Trinity Street at the turn of the century. The grocer, hardware, and china business operated here for well over a hundred years. During the alterations the shop traded at the former Foster's Bank building further along the street.

Trinity Street, showing Foster's Bank in the centre, c. 1870. Left to right: Bentley, bootmaker, Thurlborn and Sons, tailors, Foster's Bank, Deighton Bell, booksellers, and on the corner of Green Street, Metcalfe, printers.

The uneven roofline of King's Parade, 1860. Formerly part of Trumpington Street, it was given its name in 1831. Ten years before the change in name there were shops and houses on both sides. Those in front of King's College were cleared before the new screen (the wall at the front of the college) was built.

The yard of the Eagle Inn, Bene't Street, 1937. It was here in March 1953 that Francis Crick announced to his fellow customers that he and James Watson had found the secret of life. Their research into the structure of DNA would win them Nobel prizes in 1962.

Pembroke Street, 1937. On the left is Ben Hayward's cycle and motor garage. There had been a garage here from about 1901, and before that it had been the home of a cab proprietor. Today, as Henry's Café, it is possible to get service and a fill up of a different kind.

The Zoological Laboratories, formerly the Medical School and Humphrey Museum buildings, from Downing Street, 1939. On the right, in use as Liddiard's garage, is the old Corn Exchange, which was built in 1842.

The Half Moon Inn, Trumpington Street, 1872. This was soon to be demolished so that the Emmanuel Congregational church could be built. The three men standing at the top of Little St Mary's Lane are, left to right, J. Lambert, the landlord, James Hamblin Smith, who lived opposite, and a Mr Frisby, who had a business in Botolph Lane.

The Little Rose Inn, Trumpington Street, c. 1890, with Joseph Hardwick's stationer's shop to its left, and Joseph Hardwick's tailor and robe maker's shop to its right.

To obtain this view of the rebuilding of Addenbrooke's Hospital in 1865 the photographer, A. Nicholls, had climbed to the roof of the Fitzwilliam Museum. The hospital has moved but the façade remains: the building is now the newly opened Judge Institute of Management Studies.

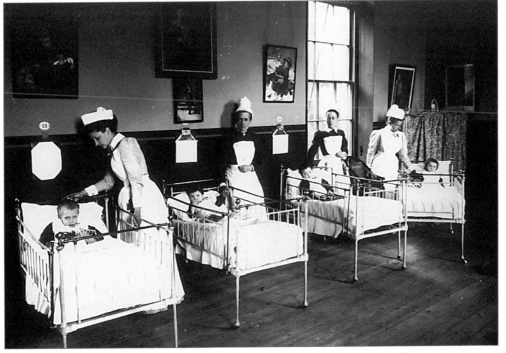

Addenbrooke's Hospital matron Mary Cureton (second left) supervises the care of children in one of the wards, July 1894.

Corn Exchange Street, 1865. Against the wall a variety of velocipedes are for hire. The relationship between cyclists and pedestrians in Cambridge can be volatile, and in 1857 it was no different. A double velocipede, ridden by undergraduates, had ploughed into a crowd watching a Punch and Judy show in Barnwell. A small child was run over, and in the weeks following letters, first deploring, then supporting, this 'unnatural and frightful invention' appeared in the local newspapers.

Members of the Cambridge University Bicycle Club about to start a race, 1870s. The first race between Oxford and Cambridge took place on 17 June 1874. Starting from Oxford at 9.50 a.m. three members of each University raced 85 miles to Cambridge. The first two home, E. Mildmay at 5.54 p.m. and J. Plunkett at 6.34 p.m., were Cambridge men.

The south side of Petty Cury, 1867. On the extreme left are the pargetted walls of the Wrestlers Inn, and then the premises of T. Holdsworth, tailor, Thomas Pont, dyer, and E. Copping, house decorator. Further along are entrances into Red Hart Yard and Falcon Yard, and yet another inn, the Red Lion, where the group of men are standing under the lion above its entrance.

Falcon Yard, looking towards Petty Cury, *c.* 1870. Twenty years earlier in 1850, the *Morning Chronicle,* writing on 'Labour and the Poor', considered the living conditions here the worst in Cambridge. The galleries were divided into apartments let at anything up to *2s* a week. One house had thirteen families in it, and in one room a man, his wife, and five children lived. One of these, a fourteen-year-old girl, was a prostitute.

The shops at the west end of Petty Cury decorated for George V's coronation, 1911. Right to left: A.R. Nichols, butcher, Morley and Co., wine and spirit merchants, and J.S. Palmer's hat and cap warehouse.

St Andrew's Street, looking towards Sidney Street and Hobson Street. If the bus belongs to The Cambridge Motor Omnibus Co. it dates the photograph to between 1905, when the company started business, and 1906, when it lost its licence owing to a series of accidents.

Police Constable Jeffrey Saddington gives directions while on point duty, 1938. Behind, on the corner of Petty Cury, is the Persil Institute, and in Sidney Street the premises of John Kittridge, tobacconist, and C.B. Warrington, butcher, can be seen.

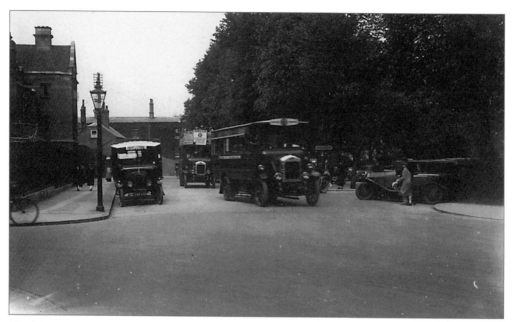

The bus station and car park in Drummer Street, which opened in November 1925. There had been strong protests at the loss of land from Christ's Pieces, the open space next to Christ's College.

In January 1938 a bus moves along Emmanuel Street, passing the shops of H.C. Payne, newsagent, P. Beales and Co., coal merchant, and W.H. Callaway, tobacconist.

The post office in St Andrew's Street, 1870s. On the left is the Inland Revenue office, then Alfred Reed, who was a jeweller, watch and clockmaker, and optician. The entrance to Post Office Terrace is through the arch. The post office would move into Petty Cury in 1885, and then back to its present position in St Andrew's Street in 1934.

St Andrew's Street, decorated for the coronation of George V, 1911. By this time the former post office was occupied by Coote and Warren, coal merchants, with part let as a University lodging house.

A crowd gathers in St Andrew's Street as smoke
envelops Ye Olde Castel Hotel, 15 August 1934.
Although the fire station was only a few doors away
the hotel was badly damaged. It was not rebuilt and
in 1937 the Regal Cinema would open on this site.

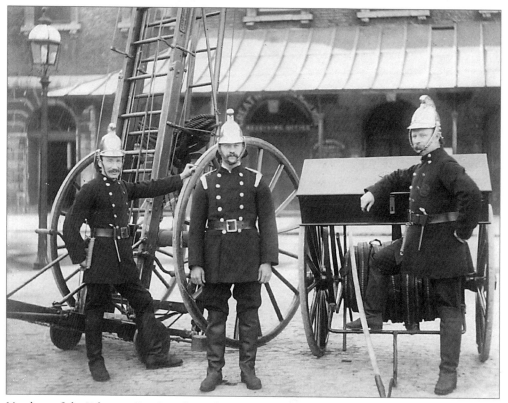

Members of the Volunteer Fire Brigade on the market-place with their equipment, *c.* 1890. Formed in
December 1874, by 1891 it consisted of a captain, lieutenant, thirty-two firemen and two turncocks. Fire
escapes were kept at the back of the Guildhall and in Warkworth Street. Ironically the brigade held their
annual dinners at Ye Olde Castel Hotel.

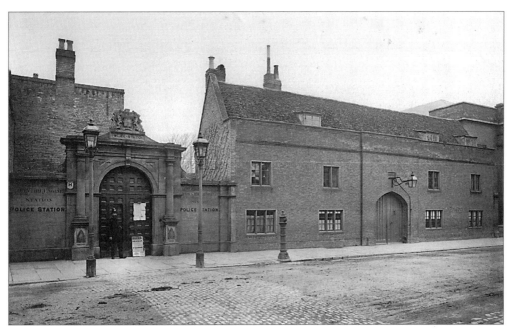

The police station and fire engine station in St Andrew's Street, *c.* 1875. The Spinning House, on the right, was founded by Thomas Hobson in the seventeenth century, to set the poor people of the town to work and act as a house of correction for 'unruly and stubborn rogues'.

St Andrew's Street, looking south, with the University Arms in the foreground. The hotel, originally built in 1834, has been added to several times. The portico, seen here extending over the pavement, was built in 1906.

Tom Hayward's charity cricket match on Parker's Piece, September 1910. Hayward, 'the famous Surrey and All-England cricketer', organised a number of matches to benefit Cambridge institutions – this year, the District Nurses' Home. Several Surrey players were included, and a large crowd watched Hayward, Hobbs, Hitch, Smith and Jephson perform. Jack Hobbs would become Cambridge's most famous cricketer. Back row, left to right: G. Smith, H. Coulson, H. Tebbutt, E. Moule, A.S. Scales, A. Titchmarsh, E.B. Darby, Reg Hayward. Third row: Dan Hayward, G. Watts, A. Hobbs, S. Speller, Tom Brown, W.C. Hunt, F.E. Collier, E. Bryan, H. Scales, W. Rumbelow, F. Addison. Second row: E. Swann, F.A. Dalton, E.E. Stubbings, F. Hayward, Tom Hayward, W.C. Smith, D.L.A. Jephson, H. Faulkner, Jack Hobbs, R. Phillips. Front row: F. Stubbings, W. Hitch, O.J. Stibbon. Tom Hayward's team of twelve players beat Frank Hayward's fourteen players. Frank stumped Tom on 79, the highest score; Jack Hobbs hit three 6s and nine 4s, and Jephson, the underarm bowler, took four wickets.

Skipping on Parker's Piece, April 1939. This Good Friday custom was common until the early years of the war. Stalls selling sweets, lemonade and toys were set up along Parkside and are visible in the background.

Cattle grazing on New Square, 1930. An open space linking Christ's Pieces with Fitzroy Street, New Square was converted into a car park in 1931 and remained so until 1983, when it was returned to grass again.

Fitzroy Street, 1939, and judging from the newspaper headlines at Rossendale and Clamp's war is imminent. Also shown is Fred Matthew's barber shop, Lovelock's fruit shop, and the Fitzroy Sweet Stores.

Another sweet shop, Harry Metcalf's, at 179 East Road, *c.* 1910.

Teachers and children at East Road Infants' School, *c*. 1900. The horses, animals, boats and dolls have also been brought out for the photographer.

The tram depot was in East Road, next to Isaac Green, builder. The trams began operating in 1880 and by 1900 were carrying over 800,000 passengers a year. However, up against fierce competition from the new and more flexible buses the company failed. The last runs were made on 18 February 1914, when, ironically, the trams were full of people having a last ride.

In May 1900, to celebrate the Relief of Mafeking during the Boer War, a huge bonfire was erected on Midsummer Common, and guarded by the police to prevent it from being set ablaze too early.

The hero of Mafeking, Sir Robert Baden-Powell, had visited Cambridge in 1908 and the first Scout Troops were formed that same year. Here are members of the 23rd Cambridge (St Matthew's) Scout Troop, *c.* 1923. Back row, left to right: L. Tilley, S. Phillips, E. Tilley, R. Eaden, W. Wolfe. Third row: A. Sansom, J. Earl, B. White, R. Curwain, C. Sansom, F. Boreham, F. Smith, S. Clark. Second row: H. Clark, J. Sansom, F. Feary, H. Wise, W. Thurbon. Front row: A. Peck, F. Taylor, F. Smith, ? Talbot, A. Gilbert, B. Morley.

A gipsy encampment on Midsummer Common, *c.* 1914, showing a variety of caravans, with children to see after and a meal to prepare.

Maids' Causeway, looking east, with Brunswick Walk visible on the left. The causeway was built with money left by Stephen Perse, who died in 1615. He also left money to found the school which still bears his name.

Christ Church, Newmarket Road, *c.* 1890. A curious looking Victorian brick copy of King's College chapel, Christ Church was built in 1839 to serve the increasing population of the Barnwell district.

The former Theatre Royal in use as a mission hall, 1890s. Religious texts surround the congregation, the principal of which, 'Where sin abounded, grace did much more abound', alludes to the building's original use. It would become well known as a theatre again, the Festival, in the 1920s and 1930s.

Station Road from Hills Road, *c.* 1900. The railway came to Cambridge in 1845, but at the insistence of the University the station and line were placed away from the town centre.

The Great Eastern Railway station frontage, *c.* 1914. The distance from the town meant good business for the hansom cabs, taxis and buses all eager to collect passengers.

The coming of the railway would lead to a marked expansion of the town eastwards, particularly with the development of the Mill Road and Romsey Town areas. Here on the corner of Devonshire Road and Mill Road stands the Great Eastern Hotel, *c.* 1900.

It was in Mill Road that Branch No. 1 of the Cambridge Co-operative Society opened. The Society had been formed in 1868 and by the end of the century the principal store was in Burleigh Street. The staff were photographed in 1908.

THE RIVER

Punts and pleasure boats on the River Cam between Garret Hostel Bridge and Trinity College Bridge,
c. 1903.

A punt, having passed the Sheep's Green bathing station, makes its way along the Cam or Granta towards Grantchester, and perhaps tea?

A hardy group of swimmers who had taken part in the Christmas morning dip at the bathing sheds, 1921. Back row, left to right: H. Bavis, E. Cherry, A. Mallion, C. Hyde, D. Lambert, J. Lavender, J. Metson, A. Broom, E. Forsdyke, E. Waits. Second row: O. Looker, A. Parsons, C. Palmer, G. Hill, A. Chater, R. Blows, F. Bye, F. Rumble, P. Northfield, R. Broom. Front row: B. Bolton, L. Weedon, W. Impey, L. Maltby, C. Driver, W. Kirkup, H. Impey, E. Impey, C. Howes.

Wrapped up for the winter, Christmas morning bathers before their dip, 1934. Charles Driver, centre front, was the bathing sheds' custodian from 1903 to 1937, and is said to have saved ninety lives. Two rows back, behind him, is Jack Overhill, who swam there every day for over sixty years.

Punting on the river between Sheep's Green and Coe Fen, 1930s.

Looking across the Mill Pool to King's Mill, early 1890s. A barge is in front of the mill, which was to be pulled down in 1928. Commercial traffic could proceed no further.

Looking from Queens' College across the Mill Pool and Laundress Green to Newnham Grange and the Old Granary, home of Professor George Darwin (son of Charles) when this photograph was taken in 1895. Darwin College would be founded here seventy years later.

Queens' College and the Silver Street Bridge, 1860. This iron bridge was erected in 1842, replacing a wooden one.

The wooden Mathematical Bridge, of Queens' College, built in 1749, and seen here in the 1860s, is so named because of its geometric design.

It was the custom, from the 1830s to the 1890s, for the college boat crews to hold a procession of boats between King's and Clare Bridges, following the May races. The boats would be decorated with club flags and flowers and a large crowd would gather to cheer the crews, as here in 1891.

The Backs seen from the entrance to King's College, *c.* 1930. From early in the seventeenth century this rough pasture and swampy ground was acquired by the colleges and turned into lawns and tree-lined walks.

A less common pastime on the river. In 1929 the river froze and skaters took to the ice opposite Trinity College library.

St John's College New Court and Bridge, 1870s. New Court, the first college buildings west of the river, are linked to Third Court by the much photographed Bridge of Sighs.

A punt glides by Bullen's boat yard where more punts are for hire, 1935. Cottages in Fisher Lane are seen in the background.

Jesus Lock and footbridge, 1890s. A higher footbridge would soon replace this one, although the river is low enough for these children to paddle.

A steam launch passes through Jesus Lock, 1894. The grassed bank between the river and Chesterton Road would be landscaped in commemoration of Queen Victoria's diamond jubilee.

Looking across the river to Chesterton Road and the Spring Brewery, *c.* 1900.

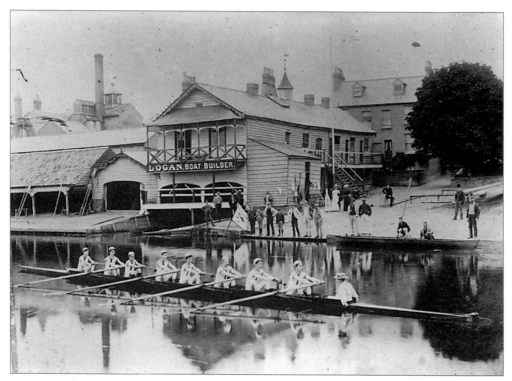

A rowing eight on the river near Logan's boathouse, *c.* 1885. Behind the boathouse, on the left, is the Spring Brewery, and on the right, Victoria House.

Several ferries linked the town with Chesterton. This one crossed from the Fort St George public house to Ferry Path. On the left is Winter's boathouse, and in the centre Caius boathouse.

In 1927 the Fort St George ferry was replaced by a footbridge, and the advantages of a footbridge over a ferry were aptly demonstrated that year when the ferry sank.

Midsummer House, 1935. Still visible on the wall of the yard is 'Callaby dog fancier'. Behind this wall in the mid-nineteenth century, undergraduates might place a wager on the time a terrier took to kill a rat, or the number of imprisoned rats a dog could kill in a fixed time.

A crew make ready at the Goldie boathouse, with the Jesus College boathouse beyond, *c*. 1910. J.H.D. Goldie of St John's and Steve Fairbairn of Jesus both played a significant part in the development of college rowing.

Emmanuel 2nd Boat crew, May 1889. The 'classic' pose for a crew, with oars and flag. In the May races this crew bumped St Catharine, Cavendish, Queens' and Downing. The names of the crew are given although there are eleven people in the photograph! Bow; K.S. Storrs, 2, T.P. Williamson, 3, R.G. Pyne, 4, P. Harrison, 5, E. Freeman, 6, N. Parsons, 7, V.P. Davis, Stroke, H. Menzies, Cox, E.W. Picton. The two inter-college races are 'The Mays', (now held in June, but originally in May), and 'The Lents', held at the end of Lent Term. Because the river is so narrow these are bumping races, with the boats chasing each other until touching or bumping. The Emmanuel crew caught four other boats over the four days of racing and so moved above them in the tables each time.

The towpath crowded with spectators as the eights race by, 1920s.

A bump is signalled by the cox of the leading boat as it is caught, 1904.

The town also holds its own bumping races and has done so since the 1860s, often with the aid of University boats, boathouses and coaches. This is the Beehive Boat Club crew which took part in the Town Races of July 1933. They bumped Pye Radio 2, College Servants 3, and Lilleys 2. Bow, C. Powley, 2, G. Matthews, 3, B. Odell, 4, T. Coulson, 5, C. Jeeves, 6, T. Abbott, 7, A. Hall, Stroke, D. Nelson, Cox, N. Plumb, President, J. Quincey, Secretary, J. Grocock.

An eight of the '99 Rowing Club, near Banham's boathouse, 1922. As the name suggests, this club was formed in the last year of the last century.

A solitary scull passes under Cutter or Pye Bridge, which replaced Dant's Ferry, seen on the left, in 1927. The boathouse is that of Emmanuel College.

A punt and pleasure boat pass the Horse Grind ferries near the Green Dragon public house, Water Street, Chesterton, 1909. One ferry was large enough to carry a horse and cart, the other pedestrians only.

A temporary bridge made out of the ferries when the river level was lowered to allow repair work on Baitsbite Lock, September 1920.

A quiet river scene at the Pike and Eel public house, Chesterton, *c.* 1905. A couple have the river to themselves.

The more hectic scene during the races. People line both banks and use the Pike and Eel ferry as the eights sweep by.

THE UNIVERSITY

Hansom cabs line up for business near the Senate House as King's College chapel and gatehouse form the back-drop, 1890s.

Trinity College Great Gate, *c*. 1900. This is the first sight of their college that newly arrived young gentlemen would have had. The figure of Henry VIII above the gateway, formerly holding a sceptre, now clasps a chair leg, as a result of a student prank.

The Head Porter and his colleague stand guard at St John's College gate and keep their eye on the luggage, *c.* 1910.

Four Trinity College bedmakers, and porters Carter and Apthorpe, 1884. The bedmakers would clean, fetch coal and water, and make the beds of undergraduates and Fellows. They were always married and elderly, so as not to tempt the young men. For many years they waited at table in the college halls, and took home food, wine and other leftovers as a perk of the job.

An undergraduate's room at Clare College, *c.* 1895. The fire-screen carries the college arms, and the cushion those of the University. The florid wallpaper is covered with framed prints and photos, and cards and trophies all add to the display.

The ivy covered walls of Peterhouse, *c.* 1860. This is the oldest college, founded in 1284.

St John's College, 1870s. In the distance is the new chapel, completed in 1869, and the lecture rooms built on the site of the old chapel. On the opposite side of the road the Divinity School has yet to be built.

St Catharine's College, *c*. 1880. A group of undergraduates lounge in Bull Court in front of the entrance to E staircase. These seventeenth-century buildings were swept away for new buildings in the 1960s.

The Bull Hotel, Trumpington Street. The notice by the door advertising the Footlights' production *The Mixture, Remixed* dates this photograph to 1894.

On 22 June 1911 the town celebrated the coronation of King George V. A service was held in King's College chapel, and here members of the Territorials and Boy Scouts form up with their colours.

Members of the Cambridge University Rifle Volunteers, with King's and Clare Colleges as a back-drop, *c.* 1860. This was the third Corps formed in the county, Cambridge Town Corps being the first. The uniform was grey with red facings.

In 1901 the head-dress of the Volunteers changed to the slouch hat, much in fashion at the time. The ribbon and feather hackle, were, as you would expect, light blue.

Degree Day, the culmination of three years' hard work? Graduates pose in front of the Senate House, where degrees are awarded. Japan and the Empire are represented, and for one at least, a celebratory cigarette is in order.

Henry Coggin, winner of the wooden spoon, 1905. By tradition this was awarded to the graduate with the lowest marks in the mathematical tripos. The trophy carries the arms of Coggin's college, Trinity.

Honorary degrees are awarded by the University as well. This procession to the Senate House, 6 June 1922, is led by the Chancellor, the Earl of Balfour, and the recipients following the University Marshall are HRH The Duke of York, W.H. Taft, former President of America (accompanied by the Lord Lieutenant C.R.W. Adeane), and two rows behind them, in the mortar-board, G.P. Hawkins, the Mayor of Cambridge.

The Earl of Balfour died in 1930 and one former Conservative Prime Minister was followed as Chancellor by another, Stanley Baldwin. Seen here in his robes, he is attended by the University Marshall and the Esquire Bedells.

The social life of the undergraduate, past and present, is a serious business, as demonstrated by this formal dinner party of about 1905.

Less seriously, this is how such events were viewed by the cartoonist Harry Moden before the First World War. But then again, the photo above was taken before the meal had begun.

A University Proctor, with a University Constable in attendance, makes a note of the offending undergraduate's name and college, outside Gonville and Caius. Elected annually, Proctors are responsible for the maintenance of good order and discipline within the University.

Four Constables, or Bulldogs, as they are more usually known, in ceremonial dress at the Senate House. Said to be chosen for their fitness, so that they were able to chase and capture wrongdoers, one of the patrolling pair might be a sprinter and the other noted for his staying power!

Rags, when undergraduates found an excuse to indulge in acts of hooliganism and vandalism, usually at the town's expense, were common at the time of local or national events of importance, particularly on 5 November. The Proctors, Bulldogs, and police were all kept busy. These two cartoons illustrate the different sides of the conflict. Left: two burly police constables arrest a chastened and diminutive undergraduate. Below: the town Chief Constable reviews his bruised and battered force after the event. A police helmet was always a much prized trophy.

In 1921 the custom began of holding a Poppy Rag Day on the Saturday nearest to 11 November, and raising money for the British Legion. This continued until 1969 when Rag Day was moved to February. These two photos were taken during the 1937 Rag Day. Right: two pirates and the *Queen Mary* collect money in St Andrew's Street. Below: the two fascist dictators Hitler and Mussolini were still considered figures of fun on Market Hill.

A degree day, and senior members of the University and their ladies gather outside the Senate House, 1913. When they were at last allowed to marry, from 1860 onwards, Fellows moved out of the colleges and had homes of their own built, particularly in the area west of the river.

This heavily retouched Christmas card shows Homeleigh in West Road, home of Sir Joseph John Thomson. Known as 'J.J.', he had won the Nobel prize for physics in 1906 (as would his son George in 1937), and he is said to have trained seven other winners at the Cavendish Laboratory.

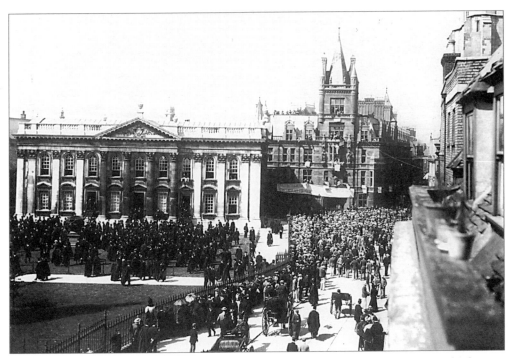

Voting on the degrees for women question, 1897. Because of the number of people involved, extra entrances were made through the windows of the Senate House. The motion was defeated, as it would be again in 1921. Women would eventually be awarded equal status in 1947.

A May Ball group at Corpus Christi College, c. 1912. The Balls are part of the celebrations to mark the end of the academic year, and for some, their final exam. At these, the young women were welcome.

The first colleges for women were Girton and Newnham. In 1887 the Liberal politician W.E. Gladstone visited Newnham College, and to mark the occasion planted a tree. Not long afterwards it was dug up by Tory undergraduates!

Newnham College students take tea together, 1887.

THE FIRST WORLD WAR

The calm before the storm: soldiers camped on Parker's Piece, near the University Arms Hotel, during the mobilisation of August 1914.

Following the declaration of war Cambridge was transformed from a quiet academic town to a bustling military centre, and every open space was filled with tents, horses and men – as here on Jesus Green, with the houses of Park Parade in the background.

Midsummer Common covered in tents belonging to soldiers of the Sixth Division, which arrived on 14 August. It was at the Mammoth Show, held here on the 4 August Bank Holiday, that many heard the first news of war, when a public call was made for men to return to duty.

The Yeomanry camp by the river near Grantchester.

Members of the North Staffordshire Regiment take the opportunity to bathe in the River Cam. The Sixth Division stayed in Cambridge for twenty-four days.

A postman watches military transport pass on Cherry Hinton Road, with the houses of Cowper Road in the background.

The 960 men of the Cambridgeshire Regiment had just returned from their annual camp when they were mobilized. Here they are leaving by train for an 'unknown destination', eventually to arrive in France in February 1915. Of the thirty officers who left with them, fifteen would die, and another seven would be wounded.

Cherry Hinton Military Hospital, *c.* 1916. One of the three hospitals established in the town, this was situated off Cherry Hinton Road, south of the fields opposite.

An ambulance train bringing wounded soldiers back to Cambridge, to be looked after at the 1st Eastern General Hospital.

The 1st Eastern General Hospital was established in Nevile's Court, Trinity College, in September 1914. The beds were placed around the cloisters.

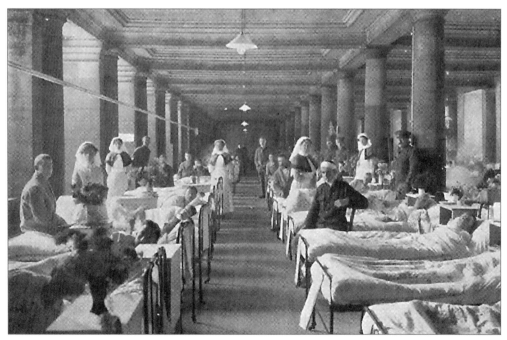

Staff and patients in Trinity College. Fortunately the weather was mild and the soldiers wounded in the earliest battles of the war were fairly comfortable.

This arrangement could only be temporary, and a large hut hospital was built on the King's and Clare playing field, seen here from the air in 1919. The houses in the foreground are along West Road.

The 1st Eastern General Hospital was eventually able to accommodate 1,500 patients, and some 62,664 passed through the hospital between August 1914 and June 1918. Of these 437 died.

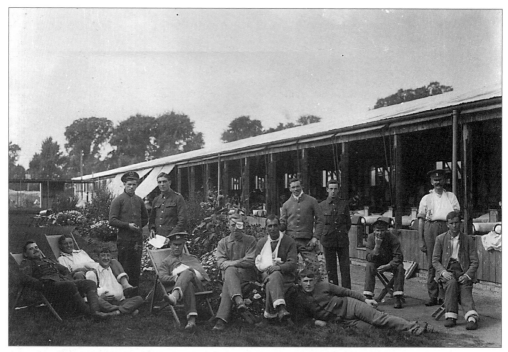

Patients, with a variety of wounds, outside one of the open-air wards. The wards, open to the south, had blinds to protect the patients from wind and rain.

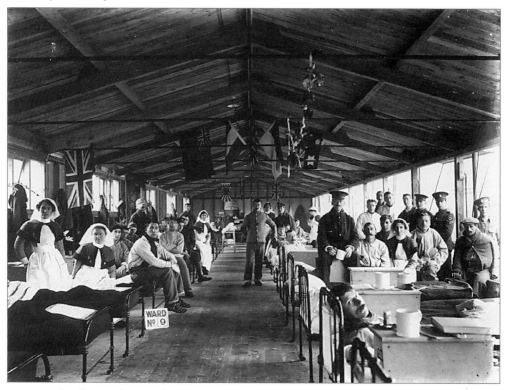

Patients and staff in ward no. 9. The open-air wards were not a great success and were eventually altered.

The war was to be 'over by Christmas', but not by this Christmas of 1916. 'Kaiser Bill' and his son 'Little Willy' make suitable subjects for snowmen.

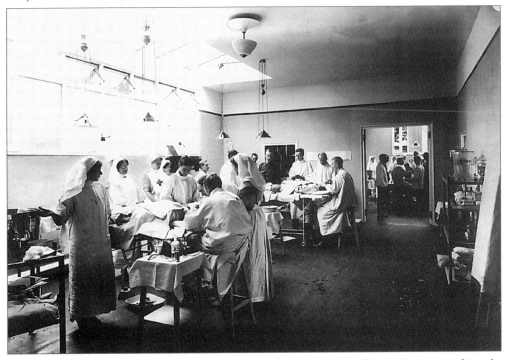

The reality of war: three patients undergoing operations in the operating theatre. You can see from the floor that their blood was being shed for King and Country.

Women were to play an ever-increasing role in the war effort, particularly on the Home Front. Here 'Lilly and Elsie' are busy fund-raising on Prisoner of War Flag Day, 18 March 1916.

As more and more men were called into the armed services, women took over their jobs at home. In 1919 the *Cambridge Independent Press* paid tribute to these women in a series of articles, including one on two of the Ortona Motor Omnibus Co. 'conductorettes', Mrs E. Maskell and Mrs M. Palmer. Their husbands both served in France.

Women window-cleaners at work on the windows of the Cambridge Automobile and Engineering Co.'s premises in Hobson Street, 1916.

Cambridge Corporation women street cleaners with the tools of their trade, 1917.

As the war progressed the number of students in the colleges declined, and many were used by the military. King's and Selwyn billeted nurses, and Clare and Caius a staff training course. Most provided quarters for officer cadet battalions and these young men soon adapted to Cambridge life. Here the Eight of No. 4 Company, 22 Officer Cadet Battalion, Magdalene College, pose in front of Pocock's boathouse; they were winners of the battalion cup in September 1917.

The Volunteer Training Corps was raised for home defence. These members of the Trumpington company were charged with protecting the Lingay Fen railway bridge.

Armoured cars on Market Hill, Christmas 1915. In contrast, behind, Boots the Chemist is advertising its Christmas cards and calendars.

On the same spot, on the afternoon of Monday 11 November 1918, a crowd celebrates the Armistice. The drizzle which fell could not dampen their enthusiasm.

Eight months after the Armistice, on 19 July 1919, Cambridge celebrated the signing of the Peace Treaty. Ex-servicemen march along St Andrew's Street to a dinner on Parker's Piece.

The Cambridgeshire war memorial, unveiled by HRH The Duke of York on 3 July 1922. Or rather the bronzed plaster cast of the figure was unveiled; the bronze itself was not ready, and arrived ten days later. The head was inspired by studies of a student at Christ's College. The memorial is the work of a Canadian, Robert Tait McKenzie.

EXTENDING THE
BOUNDARIES

The Jolly Miller's public house in Newnham Road, which after centuries of use is showing its age. It would be demolished and rebuilt in 1903.

The Perse Almshouses, on Newnham Road, 1920s. Erected here in 1886, the almshouses had formerly stood in Free School Lane, near the original Perse School.

Fen Causeway, opened in 1926 to link Newnham Road with Trumpington Road and ease traffic congestion in Silver Street.

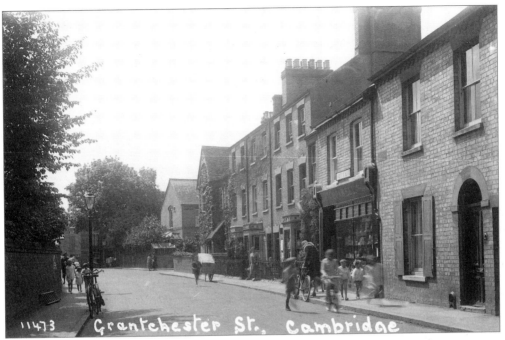

Grantchester Street, showing the post office, 1920s.

The Grantchester Street post office and shop, *c.* 1928. Before the shop frontage was built the front room of the house had served as the post office, and the counter space was cut through the hallway wall.

An Ortona bus and its driver and conductor wait in Barton Road, *c.* 1925.

A milkman makes a delivery in Marlowe Road, *c.* 1925. The houses, built between 1910 and 1912, are on land formerly owned by Corpus Christi College, where Christopher Marlowe had studied.

A happy group of youngsters in the Newnham Paddling Pool, 1933.

Bolton's Pit, from Fulbrooke Road, looking towards Gray's Farm on Barton Road, *c.* 1912. Brick making, the activity which created the pit, had begun here in the 1820s.

A horse-drawn bus collects passengers at the Wheatsheaf public house in Chesterton High Street, *c.* 1900. The landlady, Mrs Morrison, and her companion, Miss Fuller, stand in the doorway.

Victoria Bridge, seen here from Mitcham's Corner in about 1920, had opened in 1890 to link Chesterton with Cambridge.

Chesterton High Street from Chapel Street, showing Hill House and the Bleeding Heart public house, *c.* 1900.

The High Street with Radford's fish and chip shop in the foreground, 1920s. His neighbours have appeared to have their photograph taken.

Humberstone Road, virtually deserted, *c.* 1900. The De Freville estate had developed rapidly following the opening of Victoria Bridge.

W.G. Pye had begun his instrument making company in Humberstone Road in 1896. By 1932 a much larger factory in Cam Road was producing radios. This is a view of the general assembly shop.

At the end of the working day 'Pyeradians' leave the Granta Works for home. In 1932 these workers were producing 40,000 radio receivers a year.

The Pye employees also formed a variety of social and sports clubs. This is the Pye Radio Football Club team of 1931. Back row, left to right: A. Clarke, F. Boon, J. Newman, F. Clements, J. Anderson, J. Edwards, N. Bell, R. Thomas. Front row: C. Cudworth, R. Northfield, C. Ellis, S. Burton, F. Thomson, A. Kimpton, L. Ambrose.

Eastman's butcher's shop, 66 High Street, Chesterton, 1920s.

A crowd gathers to watch the new railway bridge across the river at Chesterton being moved into position, April 1930. This would be the third bridge on this site.

Cherry Hinton High Street, showing an early form of traffic calming, *c.* 1900. At this time a separate parish with little thought of becoming part of Cambridge, Cherry Hinton had a population of 1,458 in 1901.

The Five Bells public house in the High Street, 1930. It was kept by Sydney Maskall.

Cherry Hinton Road, *c.* 1910. In 1912 Cambridge would advance halfway along this road to where Perne Road and Mowbray Road are now.

Cherry Hinton Road, showing the buildings between Derby Road and Rustat Road, *c.* 1925.

The level crossing, *c.* 1920. In 1891 a petition asking for a railway station was sent to the Great Eastern Railway Co. In 1996 discussions are under way again.

Mansfield's Stores and post office, *c.* 1920.

Horace Ling's shop in the High Street, Cherry Hinton, *c.* 1910.

The lime kilns in the chalk pit in operation, 1937. The cottage at the side of the road leading into the pit had its own well.

Trumpington High Street, *c.* 1920. A bus approaches Harvey's Stores, which sells, among other items, Cadbury's Cocoa, Fry's Chocolate and Lyon's Tea.

An Automobile Association patrolman on duty near the AA box at the junction of the London and Shelford Roads, 1920s.

Blacksmiths at work in the village smithy on the High Street, Trumpington, 1890s.

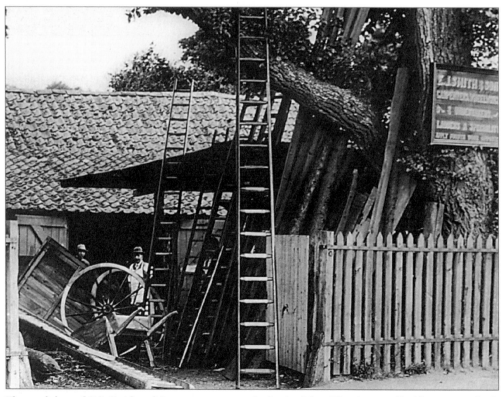

The workshop of E.J. Smith and Sons, carpenters and wheelwrights. The sign says 'Ladders a speciality', which goes without saying.

The windmill that stood at the end of Mill Road, now Long Road, 1898.

A group of schoolchildren at Trumpington School, late 1870s.

In November 1915 Miss Viola Pemberton married Dr W. Wingate. The bride's car, suitably decorated, passes children from the school, with their headmaster, Mr Robinson, on the right.

Armond Cannell, the gamekeeper on the Pemberton estate, stands by the gamekeeper's 'gibbet'. On it are displayed all the predators which might destroy game on the estate: weasels, stoats, hawks, jays and magpies.

One of Thurston's gallopers in action at Trumpington Feast, 1920.

Two less hectic forms of entertainment for the fathers of the children at the Feast: a pint and a game of bowls at the Unicorn Inn.

ACKNOWLEDGEMENTS

The principal acknowledgement is to Cambridgeshire County Council, Education, Libraries and Heritage Department, for permission to use photographs held in the Cambridgeshire Collection. A significant part of that collection is the photographic archive of the Cambridge Antiquarian Society, and I would like to thank the society and its Honorary Librarian, John Pickles, for permission to use items from this.

I would like to mention my colleagues in the Cambridgeshire Collection, who work so hard to collect material from the County's past and present for the future, particularly Katherine Heawood and Fiona Parish, with whom it is a pleasure to work. I must also thank my colleague Lynda Martin for her encouragement, advice and practical help with this volume.

Many people have given photographs to the Cambridgeshire Collection, or loaned them for copying. I thank them all.

The following is a list of those whose knowledge has contributed to this volume. I am grateful to them all, and I apologise to anyone I may have omitted: Shirley Brown, John Gray, Mike Petty, Enid Porter, Frank Reeve, Frank Stubbings.

BRITAIN IN OLD PHOTOGRAPHS

To order any of these titles please telephone our distributor, Littlehampton Book Services on 01903 721596
For a catalogue of these and our other titles please ring Regina Schinner on 01453 731114